The DeepSeek Era

A New Superpower in Artificial Intelligence

Exploring the Power and Possibilities of Advanced AI Systems

Aiden Locke

CONTENTS

Introduction 1

Chapter 1: The Genesis of DeepSeek 3

Section 1: The Birth of an Idea 3

Section 2: Building the Foundation 10

Section 3: The Launch of DeepSeek 14

Chapter 2: The Science of DeepSeek 18

Section 1: The Architecture of DeepSeek 18

Section 2: Training the AI 23

Section 3: Continuous Improvement 27

Chapter 3: DeepSeek in Action 31

Section 1: Transforming Healthcare 31

Section 2: Revolutionizing Business and Finance .. 36

Section 3: Enhancing Everyday Life 40

Chapter 4: The Ethical Dimensions of DeepSeek 45

Section 1: The Ethics of AI Development 45

Section 2: Privacy and Security Concerns 50

Section 3: Addressing Bias and Inequality 54

Chapter 5: DeepSeek and the Future of Work 58

Section 1: Automation and Job Disruption 58

Section 2: Human-AI Collaboration 62

Section 3: Preparing for the Future..........................65

Chapter 6: DeepSeek's Global Impact......................69

Section 1: Economic Transformation 69

Section 2: Cultural and Social Shifts 73

Section 3: Geopolitical Implications......................77

Chapter 7: The Road Ahead for DeepSeek...............80

Section 1: Emerging Technologies 80

Section 2: Challenges to Overcome 84

Section 3: Vision for the Future.............................89

Chapter 8: A Call to Action....................................94

Section 1: Empowering Individuals.......................94

Section 2: Building a Better Future 97

Section 3: The Legacy of DeepSeek.....................101

Introduction

Artificial Intelligence is no longer a distant dream; it is here, reshaping our world at an unprecedented pace. At the forefront of this revolution stands DeepSeek AI, an emerging powerhouse challenging Silicon Valley's long-standing dominance. This book, *The DeepSeek Era: A New Superpower in Artificial Intelligence*, explores how DeepSeek AI is redefining intelligence, pushing the boundaries of machine learning, and altering the global technological landscape.

DeepSeek AI represents more than just a company—it embodies a new wave of innovation, one that threatens to disrupt industries, economies, and even the way we perceive intelligence itself. From its origins to its groundbreaking advancements, we will uncover how DeepSeek is transforming research, business, and human-AI collaboration.

But this is not just a story of technological progress; it is a glimpse into the future. As AI systems become more autonomous, ethical concerns, geopolitical tensions, and competitive rivalries emerge. Can DeepSeek AI surpass Silicon Valley's dominance?

Will it shape a future where AI serves humanity—or one where humanity struggles to keep up?

This book is a journey into the heart of the DeepSeek AI. Welcome to the DeepSeek Era.

Chapter 1: The Genesis of DeepSeek

The story of DeepSeek is one of ambition, innovation, and perseverance. It begins with a bold vision to redefine artificial intelligence and culminates in the creation of a system that has transformed industries, inspired minds, and opened new possibilities for humanity. This chapter explores the origins of DeepSeek, from the spark of inspiration to the challenges and breakthroughs that shaped its early days.

Section 1: The Birth of an Idea

Every groundbreaking innovation begins with an idea—a moment of clarity that ignites the imagination and sets the wheels of progress in motion. For DeepSeek, that idea was born out of a desire to push the boundaries of artificial intelligence and create a system that could not only perform tasks but also learn, adapt, and collaborate with humans.

1.1 The Inspiration Behind DeepSeek

The inspiration for DeepSeek came from a combination of technological advancements, societal needs, and the personal passions of its founders.

The Technological Landscape

In the early 2010s, the field of artificial intelligence was experiencing a renaissance. Breakthroughs in deep learning, neural networks, and computational power were enabling machines to achieve feats that were once thought impossible. However, these advancements were largely confined to narrow applications. AI systems could excel at specific tasks—like playing chess or recognizing faces—but lacked the adaptability and general intelligence that would make them truly revolutionary.

The founders of DeepSeek saw this gap as an opportunity. They were inspired by the idea of creating an AI system that could go beyond narrow applications and adapt to a wide range of tasks and environments. This vision was rooted in a belief that AI could be more than just a tool—it could be a collaborator, a problem-solver, and a catalyst for human progress.

A Response to Global Challenges

The inspiration for DeepSeek was also deeply tied to the challenges facing the world at the time. Climate change, healthcare disparities, economic inequality, and other pressing issues demanded innovative solutions. The founders believed that AI had the potential to address these challenges at scale, but only if it could be developed with a focus on adaptability, ethics, and real-world impact.

For example, they envisioned an AI system that could analyze vast amounts of environmental data to predict natural disasters, optimize energy consumption, and develop sustainable solutions. They also saw the potential for AI to revolutionize healthcare by enabling early diagnosis, personalized treatment plans, and accelerated drug discovery. These aspirations became the driving force behind DeepSeek.

Personal Passions and Influences

The founders of DeepSeek were not just technologists; they were dreamers, philosophers, and humanists. They drew inspiration from a wide range of disciplines, including neuroscience, psychology, and even art. One founder, a neuroscientist by training, was fascinated by the parallels between the human brain and artificial neural networks. Another, a software engineer with a background in philosophy, was deeply interested in the ethical implications of AI and its potential to enhance human flourishing.

These diverse perspectives converged to create a shared vision: an AI system that was not only intelligent but also aligned with human values and capable of contributing to the greater good. This vision would become the guiding principle of DeepSeek.

1.2 The Founders' Vision: A New Era of AI

The founders of DeepSeek were united by a bold and ambitious vision: to usher in a new era of artificial intelligence that would redefine the relationship between humans and machines. This vision was rooted in three core principles: adaptability, collaboration, and ethical responsibility.

Adaptability: Beyond Narrow AI

At the heart of the founders' vision was the idea of creating an AI system that could go beyond narrow applications and adapt to a wide range of tasks and environments. They envisioned an AI that could learn from experience, generalize knowledge across domains, and continuously improve over time.

This focus on adaptability was inspired by the limitations of existing AI systems, which often required extensive retraining or reprogramming to handle new tasks. The founders believed that by developing AI with a more flexible and dynamic architecture, they could create a system that was truly versatile and capable of tackling complex, real-world problems.

Collaboration: AI as a Partner, Not a Replacement

The founders were acutely aware of the fears and misconceptions surrounding AI, particularly the notion that it would replace human jobs and diminish human agency. They sought to counter this narrative by positioning DeepSeek as a collaborator rather than a competitor.

Their vision was to create an AI system that could augment human capabilities, enabling people to achieve more than they could on their own. For example, they imagined DeepSeek assisting doctors in diagnosing diseases, helping scientists analyze complex data, and empowering educators to personalize learning experiences. By emphasizing collaboration, the founders aimed to build trust and foster a positive relationship between humans and AI.

Ethical Responsibility: AI for Good

From the outset, the founders were committed to developing DeepSeek with a strong ethical foundation. They recognized that AI had the potential to cause harm if not designed and deployed responsibly. To address this, they established a set of guiding principles that prioritized transparency, fairness, and accountability.

One of their key ethical commitments was to ensure that DeepSeek would be free from bias and discrimination. They invested heavily in developing algorithms that could identify and mitigate biases in data, as well as mechanisms for human oversight and intervention. They also envisioned DeepSeek as a tool for promoting social good, with applications in areas like healthcare, education, and environmental sustainability.

1.3 Early Challenges and Breakthroughs

The journey from vision to reality was far from smooth. The early days of DeepSeek were marked by a series of challenges that tested the founders' resolve and ingenuity. However, these challenges also led to breakthroughs that would shape the future of the project.

Technical Hurdles

One of the first challenges the team faced was developing an AI architecture that could achieve the level of adaptability they envisioned. Existing models were either too rigid or too resource-intensive to scale effectively. The team spent countless hours experimenting with different approaches, from reinforcement learning to modular neural networks.

A major breakthrough came when they developed a novel algorithm that allowed DeepSeek to transfer knowledge from one domain to another. This innovation, inspired by the way humans learn, enabled the AI to apply insights from one task to solve problems in a completely different context. It was a game-changer that laid the groundwork for DeepSeek's versatility.

Resource Constraints

In the early stages, the team operated on a shoestring budget, relying on grants, personal savings, and the goodwill of early supporters. They worked out of a small office space, often pulling all-nighters to meet deadlines. Despite these constraints, they remained fiercely committed to their vision.

A turning point came when they secured their first major investment from a venture capital firm that shared their belief in the potential of AI. This funding allowed them to expand the team, acquire better infrastructure, and accelerate the development of DeepSeek.

Building the Team

Another challenge was assembling a team that shared the founders' vision and had the skills to bring it to life. They sought out individuals who were not only technically proficient but also passionate about the ethical and societal implications of AI.

One of their early hires was a data scientist who had previously worked on AI projects in the healthcare sector. Her expertise in handling sensitive data and ensuring privacy was instrumental in shaping DeepSeek's ethical framework. Another key addition was a software engineer with a background in robotics, whose insights helped make DeepSeek more adaptable and user-friendly.

Early Successes

Despite the challenges, the team achieved several early successes that validated their vision. One of the first was a prototype that could analyze medical images with remarkable accuracy, outperforming existing systems. This prototype caught the attention of healthcare providers and demonstrated the potential of DeepSeek to make a real-world impact.

Another milestone was the development of a natural language processing module that could understand and generate human-like text. This breakthrough opened up new possibilities for applications in customer service, education, and content creation.

Section 2: Building the Foundation

With the initial vision in place and early breakthroughs achieved, the team turned their attention to building the foundation for DeepSeek. This involved developing the core technologies, assembling a world-class team, and securing the resources needed to turn their vision into reality.

2.1 The Core Technologies Behind DeepSeek

At the heart of DeepSeek's success were the cutting-edge technologies that powered its capabilities. These technologies were carefully selected and developed to align with the founders' vision of adaptability, collaboration, and ethical responsibility.

Neural Networks and Deep Learning

DeepSeek's architecture was built on the foundation of neural networks and deep learning. These technologies enabled the AI to process vast amounts of data, identify patterns, and make predictions with a high degree of accuracy. The team focused on developing models that could learn from limited data and generalize across tasks, a key requirement for achieving adaptability.

Transfer Learning

One of the most significant innovations was the integration of transfer learning into DeepSeek's architecture. This approach allowed the AI to apply knowledge gained from one task to solve problems in a different domain. For example, a model trained to recognize objects in images could be adapted to analyze medical scans or interpret satellite imagery.

Ethical AI Frameworks

To ensure that DeepSeek operated in an ethical and responsible manner, the team developed a suite of tools and frameworks for bias detection, fairness, and transparency. These included algorithms for identifying and mitigating biases in training data, as well as mechanisms for explaining the AI's decision-making process to users.

2.2 Assembling the Dream Team: Innovators and Engineers

The success of DeepSeek was as much about the people behind it as the technology itself. The founders recognized early on that building a world-class AI system required a diverse and talented team.

Recruiting Top Talent

The team sought out individuals with expertise in a wide range of disciplines, from machine learning and data science to ethics and human-computer interaction. They prioritized candidates who shared their passion for innovation and their commitment to ethical AI.

Fostering a Collaborative Culture

The founders placed a strong emphasis on collaboration and open communication. They created an environment where team members felt empowered to share ideas, challenge assumptions, and take risks. This culture of innovation was instrumental in driving the project forward.

Mentorship and Growth

The team also invested in mentorship and professional development, ensuring that every member had the opportunity to grow and contribute to their fullest potential. This approach not only strengthened the team but also helped attract top talent from around the world.

2.3 Funding and Early Support: Turning Vision into Reality

Securing the resources needed to develop DeepSeek was a major challenge, but the team's persistence and vision eventually paid off.

Early Funding Challenges

In the early days, the team relied on a combination of personal savings, grants, and small investments from friends and family. While these resources were limited, they allowed the team to make progress and demonstrate the potential of their vision.

Securing Major Investment

A turning point came when the team secured their first major investment from a venture capital firm that shared their belief in the potential of AI. This funding provided the resources needed to expand the team, acquire better infrastructure, and accelerate development.

Building Strategic Partnerships

The team also forged strategic partnerships with academic institutions, industry leaders, and nonprofit organizations. These partnerships provided access to valuable data, expertise, and resources, as well as opportunities to test and refine DeepSeek in real-world applications.

Section 3: The Launch of DeepSeek

After years of hard work and dedication, the team was ready to unveil DeepSeek to the world. The launch marked the culmination of their efforts and the beginning of a new chapter in the story of artificial intelligence.

3.1 The First Prototype: A Game-Changer in AI

The first prototype of DeepSeek was a testament to the team's vision and ingenuity. It showcased the AI's ability to adapt to a wide range of tasks, from analyzing medical images to generating human-like text.

A Versatile and Powerful System

The prototype demonstrated DeepSeek's versatility and power, earning praise from early users and industry experts. It was a clear indication that the team's vision of adaptable, collaborative, and ethical AI was within reach.

Real-World Impact

The prototype also had a tangible impact on real-world problems. For example, it was used to analyze medical scans and assist doctors in diagnosing diseases, leading to faster and more accurate diagnoses.

3.2 Initial Applications and Industry Reactions

The launch of DeepSeek generated significant interest and excitement across industries. Early applications demonstrated the AI's potential to transform healthcare, finance, education, and more.

Healthcare

In healthcare, DeepSeek was used to analyze medical images, predict patient outcomes, and accelerate drug discovery. These applications had the potential to save lives and reduce costs, earning praise from healthcare providers and researchers.

Finance

In finance, DeepSeek was used to analyze market trends, detect fraud, and optimize investment strategies. These applications demonstrated the AI's ability to handle complex data and make informed decisions in real time.

Education

In education, DeepSeek was used to personalize learning experiences, provide real-time feedback, and assist teachers in developing customized lesson plans. These applications highlighted the AI's potential to enhance learning and improve outcomes for students.

3.3 Lessons Learned from the Early Days

The launch of DeepSeek was a major milestone, but it was also a learning experience. The team gained valuable insights that would shape the future of the project.

The Importance of Adaptability

One of the key lessons was the importance of adaptability—not just in the AI itself, but in the team's approach to development. The ability to pivot, experiment, and learn from failures was critical to the project's success.

The Power of Collaboration

The team also learned the value of collaboration, both within the team and with external partners. By working together and leveraging diverse perspectives, they were able to overcome challenges and achieve breakthroughs.

A Commitment to Ethical AI

Finally, the team reaffirmed their commitment to ethical AI. They recognized that building trust and ensuring responsible use of the technology were essential to its long-term success.

Chapter 2: The Science of DeepSeek

At the heart of DeepSeek lies a sophisticated blend of cutting-edge technologies and innovative methodologies that enable it to perform at the forefront of artificial intelligence. This chapter delves into the technical and scientific innovations that power DeepSeek, exploring its architecture, training processes, and mechanisms for continuous improvement. By understanding the science behind DeepSeek, we gain insight into how it achieves its remarkable capabilities and why it stands out in the crowded field of AI.

Section 1: The Architecture of DeepSeek

The architecture of DeepSeek is the foundation upon which its capabilities are built. It combines advanced neural networks, scalable data processing systems, and unique algorithms to create an AI system that is both powerful and adaptable.

1.1 Neural Networks and Deep Learning: The Backbone of DeepSeek

Neural networks and deep learning form the core of DeepSeek's architecture, enabling it to process complex data, recognize patterns, and make decisions with remarkable accuracy.

The Basics of Neural Networks

Neural networks are computational models inspired by the structure and function of the human brain. They consist of layers of interconnected nodes, or "neurons," that work together to process input data and generate output. Each neuron performs a simple computation, but when combined in layers, they can model highly complex relationships.

DeepSeek leverages deep neural networks, which are characterized by their multiple hidden layers. These layers allow the system to learn hierarchical representations of data, capturing both low-level features (like edges in an image) and high-level abstractions (like objects or concepts).

Deep Learning: The Engine of DeepSeek

Deep learning is a subset of machine learning that focuses on training deep neural networks. It has revolutionized AI by enabling systems to learn directly from raw data, without the need for manual feature engineering.

DeepSeek's deep learning capabilities allow it to excel in a wide range of tasks, from image and speech recognition to natural language processing. For example, in healthcare, DeepSeek can analyze medical images to detect abnormalities, while in finance, it can process vast amounts of transaction data to identify fraudulent activity.

Custom Architectures for Specific Tasks

One of DeepSeek's strengths is its ability to tailor its neural network architectures to specific tasks. For instance, convolutional neural networks (CNNs) are used for image-related tasks, while recurrent neural networks (RNNs) and transformers are employed for sequential data like text and speech. This flexibility ensures that DeepSeek can deliver optimal performance across diverse applications.

1.2 Data Processing and Scalability: Handling the Information Deluge

DeepSeek's ability to process and analyze vast amounts of data is a key factor in its success. Its architecture is designed to handle the "information deluge" of the modern world, ensuring scalability, efficiency, and reliability.

Data Ingestion and Preprocessing

Before data can be used to train DeepSeek, it must be ingested and preprocessed. This involves cleaning the data, removing noise, and transforming it into a format suitable for analysis. DeepSeek employs automated pipelines to streamline this process, ensuring that data is ready for training in a timely manner.

Distributed Computing for Scalability

To handle the massive volumes of data required for training, DeepSeek relies on distributed computing systems. These systems divide the workload across multiple machines, enabling parallel processing and significantly reducing training times. Technologies like Apache Hadoop and TensorFlow are integral to this process.

Real-Time Data Processing

In addition to batch processing, DeepSeek is capable of real-time data processing, allowing it to analyze streaming data and make decisions on the fly. This capability is particularly valuable in applications like autonomous driving, where split-second decisions can mean the difference between safety and disaster.

1.3 Unique Algorithms: What Sets DeepSeek Apart

While neural networks and deep learning are foundational to DeepSeek, it is the system's unique algorithms that truly set it apart from other AI systems. These algorithms enhance its adaptability, efficiency, and ethical robustness.

Transfer Learning Algorithms

One of DeepSeek's most innovative features is its use of transfer learning algorithms. These algorithms enable the system to apply knowledge gained from one task to solve problems in a different domain. For example, a model trained to recognize objects in images can be adapted to analyze medical scans or interpret satellite imagery.

Transfer learning not only reduces the need for large amounts of labeled data but also accelerates the training process, making DeepSeek more efficient and cost-effective.

Explainability Algorithms

DeepSeek incorporates explainability algorithms that provide insights into its decision-making process. These algorithms generate human-readable explanations for the system's predictions, helping users understand how and why a particular decision was made.

Explainability is particularly important in high-stakes applications like healthcare and finance, where transparency and accountability are critical. By making its decisions interpretable, DeepSeek builds trust and ensures responsible use.

Ethical AI Algorithms

To address concerns about bias and fairness, DeepSeek employs ethical AI algorithms that detect and mitigate biases in training data. These algorithms ensure that the system's predictions are fair and unbiased, regardless of the demographic characteristics of the data.

For example, in hiring applications, DeepSeek's ethical AI algorithms can identify and correct for biases related to gender, race, or age, ensuring that candidates are evaluated solely on their qualifications.

Section 2: Training the AI

Training is the process by which DeepSeek learns from data and develops its capabilities. This section explores the key components of DeepSeek's training process, from data collection and curation to the role of reinforcement learning and the challenges of overcoming bias.

2.1 Data Collection and Curation: Fueling the AI Engine

Data is the lifeblood of any AI system, and DeepSeek is no exception. The quality and quantity of data used for training directly impact the system's performance and reliability.

Diverse and Representative Data

DeepSeek's training data is carefully curated to ensure diversity and representativeness. This means including data from a wide range of sources, contexts, and demographics to avoid biases and ensure that the system performs well across different scenarios.

For example, in healthcare, DeepSeek's training data includes medical images from patients of different ages, genders, and ethnicities, ensuring that the system can accurately diagnose conditions for all populations.

Data Augmentation Techniques

To maximize the utility of available data, DeepSeek employs data augmentation techniques that artificially expand the dataset. These techniques include rotating, cropping, and flipping images, as well as adding noise or altering lighting conditions.

Data augmentation not only increases the size of the training dataset but also enhances the system's ability to generalize to new, unseen data.

Ethical Data Collection Practices

DeepSeek adheres to strict ethical guidelines for data collection, ensuring that data is obtained with informed consent and used in a manner that respects privacy and confidentiality. These practices are essential for building trust and ensuring compliance with regulations like GDPR.

2.2 The Role of Reinforcement Learning in DeepSeek

Reinforcement learning (RL) is a powerful training paradigm that enables DeepSeek to learn through trial and error, guided by rewards and penalties.

How Reinforcement Learning Works

In reinforcement learning, the AI interacts with an environment and receives feedback in the form of rewards or penalties based on its actions. Over time, the system learns to maximize rewards by identifying the most effective strategies.

DeepSeek uses RL in applications like robotics, where the system must learn to perform complex tasks through repeated practice. For example, a robot trained with RL can learn to navigate a cluttered environment by receiving rewards for avoiding obstacles and penalties for collisions.

Combining RL with Supervised Learning

DeepSeek often combines reinforcement learning with supervised learning to accelerate the training process. In this hybrid approach, the system is first trained on labeled data using supervised learning and then fine-tuned using RL to optimize performance.

This combination allows DeepSeek to leverage the strengths of both paradigms, achieving faster and more efficient training.

2.3 Overcoming Bias: Ensuring Fairness and Accuracy

Bias is a major challenge in AI development, as biased training data can lead to unfair or inaccurate predictions. DeepSeek employs a range of techniques to identify and mitigate bias, ensuring that its decisions are fair and reliable.

Bias Detection Algorithms

DeepSeek's bias detection algorithms analyze training data for patterns of bias, such as underrepresentation of certain groups or correlations between protected attributes and outcomes. These algorithms flag potential biases, allowing developers to address them before the system is deployed.

Fairness-Aware Training

To ensure fairness, DeepSeek incorporates fairness-aware training techniques that explicitly optimize for equitable outcomes. These techniques adjust the training process to minimize disparities in performance across different demographic groups.

For example, in hiring applications, fairness-aware training ensures that DeepSeek evaluates candidates equally, regardless of gender or ethnicity.

Continuous Monitoring and Auditing

Bias mitigation is an ongoing process, and DeepSeek continuously monitors its performance to identify and address new biases that may emerge over time. Regular audits are conducted to ensure that the system remains fair and unbiased in real-world applications.

Section 3: Continuous Improvement

DeepSeek is not a static system; it is designed to evolve and improve over time. This section explores the mechanisms that enable continuous improvement, from iterative learning to feedback loops and human oversight.

3.1 Iterative Learning: How DeepSeek Evolves Over Time

Iterative learning is a key feature of DeepSeek, allowing the system to refine its models and improve its performance with each iteration.

Incremental Model Updates

DeepSeek regularly updates its models with new data, ensuring that its predictions remain accurate and up-to-date. These incremental updates are performed without the need for retraining from scratch, making the process efficient and cost-effective.

Adapting to Changing Environments

DeepSeek's iterative learning capabilities enable it to adapt to changing environments and evolving user needs. For example, in e-commerce, the system can adjust its recommendations based on shifting consumer preferences and trends.

3.2 Feedback Loops and Real-World Applications

Feedback loops are essential for DeepSeek's continuous improvement, providing the system with valuable insights from real-world applications.

User Feedback

DeepSeek actively solicits feedback from users, incorporating their input to refine its models and enhance its performance. This feedback is particularly valuable in applications like customer service, where user satisfaction is a key metric of success.

Performance Metrics

DeepSeek tracks a range of performance metrics, such as accuracy, precision, and recall, to evaluate its effectiveness and identify areas for improvement. These metrics are analyzed regularly to ensure that the system meets its performance goals.

3.3 The Role of Human Oversight in AI Development

While DeepSeek is highly autonomous, human oversight remains a critical component of its development and deployment.

Ethical Review Boards

DeepSeek's development process includes ethical review boards that evaluate the system's impact on society and ensure that it aligns with ethical principles. These boards provide guidance on issues like bias, privacy, and accountability.

Human-in-the-Loop Systems

In high-stakes applications, DeepSeek employs human-in-the-loop systems that combine the strengths of AI and human expertise. For example, in healthcare, doctors review DeepSeek's diagnoses to ensure accuracy and provide additional context.

Transparency and Accountability

DeepSeek is committed to transparency and accountability, providing users with clear explanations of its decisions and the rationale behind them. This transparency builds trust and ensures that the system is used responsibly.

Chapter 3: DeepSeek in Action

DeepSeek is not just a theoretical marvel; it is a practical powerhouse that is transforming industries and improving lives. This chapter explores the real-world applications of DeepSeek across healthcare, business, finance, and everyday life. Through case studies and examples, we will see how DeepSeek's capabilities are being harnessed to solve complex problems, drive innovation, and create value.

Section 1: Transforming Healthcare

Healthcare is one of the most promising and impactful areas of application for DeepSeek. By leveraging its advanced AI capabilities, DeepSeek is revolutionizing the way diseases are diagnosed, drugs are developed, and treatments are personalized.

1.1 Diagnosing Diseases with Precision

Accurate and timely diagnosis is critical for effective healthcare, and DeepSeek is making significant strides in this area.

Medical Imaging Analysis

DeepSeek's ability to analyze medical images with remarkable accuracy has transformed diagnostics. For example, in radiology, DeepSeek can analyze X-rays, MRIs, and CT scans to detect abnormalities such as tumors, fractures, and infections.

A case study from a leading hospital demonstrated how DeepSeek reduced the time required to diagnose lung cancer from weeks to minutes. By analyzing thousands of chest X-rays, the system identified early-stage tumors that were missed by human radiologists, enabling timely intervention and improving patient outcomes.

Pathology and Histology

In pathology, DeepSeek is being used to analyze tissue samples and detect diseases like cancer. The system can identify subtle patterns and anomalies in histology slides, providing pathologists with valuable insights and reducing the risk of misdiagnosis.

For instance, a pathology lab integrated DeepSeek into its workflow and reported a 30% increase in diagnostic accuracy. The system's ability to process large volumes of data quickly also allowed the lab to handle a higher caseload without compromising quality.

Early Detection of Chronic Diseases

DeepSeek is also being used to predict and detect chronic diseases like diabetes and cardiovascular conditions. By analyzing patient data, including medical history, lifestyle factors, and genetic information, the system can identify individuals at risk and recommend preventive measures.

In one pilot program, DeepSeek analyzed data from wearable devices to detect early signs of heart disease. The system flagged at-risk patients, enabling healthcare providers to intervene before the condition worsened.

1.2 Drug Discovery and Development

The process of discovering and developing new drugs is time-consuming and expensive, but DeepSeek is streamlining this process and accelerating innovation.

Identifying Potential Drug Candidates

DeepSeek's ability to analyze vast amounts of biological and chemical data has made it a valuable tool for identifying potential drug candidates. The system can predict how different compounds will interact with biological targets, helping researchers prioritize the most promising candidates for further testing.

A pharmaceutical company used DeepSeek to screen millions of compounds for a new cancer drug. The system identified several potential candidates, one of which is now in clinical trials. This process, which would have taken years using traditional methods, was completed in just a few months.

Optimizing Clinical Trials

DeepSeek is also being used to optimize clinical trials by identifying suitable participants, predicting outcomes, and monitoring progress. This reduces the time and cost of trials while improving their success rates.

In a recent clinical trial for a new Alzheimer's drug, DeepSeek analyzed patient data to identify individuals most likely to benefit from the treatment. The system also monitored participants in real time, providing researchers with valuable insights and enabling them to make adjustments as needed.

Repurposing Existing Drugs

Another exciting application of DeepSeek is drug repurposing, where existing drugs are used to treat new conditions. By analyzing data from previous studies, DeepSeek can identify drugs that may be effective for new indications.

For example, DeepSeek identified a drug originally developed for hypertension as a potential treatment for Parkinson's disease. This discovery has opened up new avenues for research and could lead to faster, more cost-effective treatments.

1.3 Personalized Medicine: Tailoring Treatments to Individuals

Personalized medicine is the future of healthcare, and DeepSeek is at the forefront of this revolution.

Genomic Analysis

DeepSeek's ability to analyze genomic data is enabling personalized treatments based on an individual's genetic makeup. By identifying genetic mutations and variations, the system can recommend targeted therapies that are more effective and have fewer side effects.

In one case, DeepSeek analyzed the genome of a cancer patient and identified a rare mutation that made the tumor resistant to standard treatments. The system recommended a targeted therapy that successfully shrank the tumor, saving the patient's life.

Predictive Analytics for Treatment Outcomes

DeepSeek's predictive analytics capabilities are also being used to forecast treatment outcomes and guide decision-making. By analyzing patient data, the system can predict how individuals will respond to different treatments, helping doctors choose the best course of action.

For example, in a study of patients with depression, DeepSeek analyzed data from electronic health records to predict which patients would benefit from cognitive-behavioral therapy versus medication. The system's predictions were 85% accurate, significantly improving treatment outcomes.

Personalized Health Plans

DeepSeek is also being used to create personalized health plans that take into account an individual's medical history, lifestyle, and preferences. These plans include recommendations for diet, exercise, and preventive care, helping individuals achieve their health goals.

A wellness program integrated DeepSeek into its platform and reported a 40% increase in participant engagement. The system's personalized recommendations were credited with driving this success.

Section 2: Revolutionizing Business and Finance

DeepSeek is not just transforming healthcare; it is also revolutionizing the way businesses operate and financial decisions are made.

2.1 Predictive Analytics and Market Trends

In the fast-paced world of business, staying ahead of market trends is critical, and DeepSeek's predictive analytics capabilities are proving invaluable.

Demand Forecasting

DeepSeek is being used to predict consumer demand and optimize inventory management. By analyzing historical sales data, market trends, and external factors like weather and holidays, the system can forecast demand with remarkable accuracy.

A retail chain used DeepSeek to optimize its inventory levels, reducing stockouts by 25% and excess inventory by 15%. This resulted in significant cost savings and improved customer satisfaction.

Market Trend Analysis

DeepSeek's ability to analyze vast amounts of data from social media, news, and financial reports is helping businesses identify emerging trends and capitalize on new opportunities.

For example, a fashion brand used DeepSeek to analyze social media posts and identify a growing interest in sustainable fashion. The company quickly launched a new line of eco-friendly products, which became a bestseller.

Investment Strategies

In finance, DeepSeek is being used to develop data-driven investment strategies. By analyzing market data, economic indicators, and company performance, the system can identify promising investment opportunities and optimize portfolios.

A hedge fund integrated DeepSeek into its trading platform and reported a 20% increase in returns. The system's ability to process and analyze data in real time was credited with driving this success.

2.2 Automating Customer Service and Support

Customer service is a critical component of business success, and DeepSeek is helping companies deliver faster, more efficient support.

Chatbots and Virtual Assistants

DeepSeek's natural language processing capabilities are being used to power chatbots and virtual assistants that can handle a wide range of customer inquiries. These systems provide instant responses, reducing wait times and improving customer satisfaction.

A telecommunications company deployed a DeepSeek-powered chatbot and reported a 30% reduction in call center volume. The chatbot handled routine inquiries, freeing up human agents to focus on more complex issues.

Sentiment Analysis

DeepSeek's sentiment analysis capabilities are also being used to monitor customer feedback and identify areas for improvement. By analyzing reviews, social media posts, and survey responses, the system can gauge customer sentiment and provide actionable insights.

For example, a hotel chain used DeepSeek to analyze guest reviews and identify common complaints. The company addressed these issues, resulting in a 15% increase in guest satisfaction scores.

2.3 Fraud Detection and Risk Management

Fraud and risk management are major challenges for businesses, and DeepSeek is helping companies address these issues with greater efficiency and accuracy.

Fraud Detection

DeepSeek's ability to analyze transaction data in real time is making it a powerful tool for fraud detection. The system can identify suspicious patterns and flag potentially fraudulent activity, enabling companies to take immediate action.

A financial institution integrated DeepSeek into its fraud detection system and reported a 40% reduction in fraudulent transactions. The system's ability to learn and adapt over time was credited with driving this success.

Risk Assessment

DeepSeek is also being used to assess and manage risk in areas like lending, insurance, and supply chain management. By analyzing data from multiple sources, the system can identify potential risks and recommend mitigation strategies.

For example, an insurance company used DeepSeek to analyze claims data and identify high-risk policies. The company adjusted its underwriting criteria, resulting in a 20% reduction in claims payouts.

Section 3: Enhancing Everyday Life

DeepSeek is not just transforming industries; it is also enhancing everyday life by making homes smarter, education more personalized, and entertainment more engaging.

3.1 Smart Homes and IoT Integration

DeepSeek is at the heart of the smart home revolution, enabling seamless integration of IoT devices and creating more convenient, efficient, and secure living environments.

Home Automation

DeepSeek's ability to learn and adapt is being used to automate routine tasks like adjusting thermostats, controlling lighting, and managing appliances. These systems can be controlled via voice commands or mobile apps, providing users with greater convenience and control.

For example, a smart home system powered by DeepSeek learned a family's daily routines and automatically adjusted the temperature and lighting to match their preferences. This resulted in a 20% reduction in energy consumption.

Security and Surveillance

DeepSeek is also being used to enhance home security by analyzing data from cameras, sensors, and alarms. The system can detect unusual activity and alert homeowners or security personnel in real time.

A security company integrated DeepSeek into its surveillance system and reported a 50% reduction in false alarms. The system's ability to distinguish between normal activity and potential threats was credited with driving this success.

3.2 AI in Education: Personalized Learning Experiences

Education is another area where DeepSeek is making a significant impact, enabling personalized learning experiences that cater to the unique needs of each student.

Adaptive Learning Platforms

DeepSeek's adaptive learning platforms analyze student performance and tailor content to their individual needs. These platforms provide personalized recommendations, helping students learn at their own pace and achieve better outcomes.

A school district implemented a DeepSeek-powered learning platform and reported a 25% increase in student test scores. The system's ability to identify and address learning gaps was credited with driving this success.

Virtual Tutors

DeepSeek is also being used to develop virtual tutors that provide personalized support to students. These tutors can answer questions, provide feedback, and offer guidance, helping students stay on track and achieve their goals.

For example, a virtual tutor powered by DeepSeek helped a struggling student improve their math skills by providing step-by-step explanations and practice problems. The student's grades improved significantly, and they gained confidence in their abilities.

3.3 Entertainment and Creativity: AI as a Collaborator

DeepSeek is not just a tool for solving problems; it is also a collaborator that is enhancing creativity and entertainment.

Content Creation

DeepSeek's ability to generate text, images, and music is being used to create new forms of content. For example, the system can write articles, compose music, and design graphics, providing creators with new tools and inspiration.

A media company used DeepSeek to generate news articles and reported a 30% increase in content production. The system's ability to analyze data and generate high-quality content was credited with driving this success.

Gaming and Virtual Reality

DeepSeek is also being used to enhance gaming and virtual reality experiences. The system can create realistic environments, generate dynamic storylines, and adapt gameplay to the preferences of individual players.

For example, a game developer integrated DeepSeek into its virtual reality platform and reported a 40% increase in player engagement. The system's ability to create immersive and personalized experiences was credited with driving this success.

Chapter 4: The Ethical Dimensions of DeepSeek

Artificial intelligence has the potential to revolutionize industries, improve lives, and solve some of the world's most pressing challenges. However, with great power comes great responsibility. As DeepSeek continues to advance, it is essential to critically examine the ethical implications of its technology. This chapter explores the moral and societal dimensions of DeepSeek, focusing on the ethics of AI development, privacy and security concerns, and the challenges of bias and inequality. By addressing these issues, we can ensure that DeepSeek is developed and deployed in a way that benefits humanity while minimizing harm.

Section 1: The Ethics of AI Development

The development of AI systems like DeepSeek raises profound ethical questions about innovation, autonomy, and transparency. How do we balance the pursuit of technological progress with the need to protect human values and rights?

1.1 Balancing Innovation with Responsibility

Innovation is at the core of DeepSeek's mission, but it must be pursued responsibly. The rapid pace of AI development often outstrips the ability of society to fully understand and regulate its implications.

The Dual-Use Dilemma

One of the key ethical challenges in AI development is the dual-use dilemma, where technology designed for beneficial purposes can also be used for harm. For example, DeepSeek's natural language processing capabilities could be used to create educational tools or to generate disinformation and manipulate public opinion.

To address this, DeepSeek's developers have implemented strict ethical guidelines and oversight mechanisms. These include conducting risk assessments for new applications, engaging with stakeholders to identify potential misuse, and establishing protocols for responding to ethical concerns.

The Precautionary Principle

The precautionary principle suggests that if an action or technology has the potential to cause harm, even in the absence of scientific consensus, precautionary measures should be taken. DeepSeek's development process incorporates this principle by prioritizing safety and ethical considerations over speed and profit.

For instance, before deploying DeepSeek in high-stakes applications like healthcare or criminal justice, the team conducts extensive testing to ensure the system's reliability and fairness. This cautious approach helps mitigate risks and build public trust.

Corporate Social Responsibility

DeepSeek's developers recognize that they have a responsibility not only to their shareholders but also to society at large. This commitment to corporate social responsibility is reflected in their efforts to use AI for social good, such as developing tools to address climate change, improve education, and enhance healthcare access.

1.2 The Debate Over AI Autonomy

As AI systems like DeepSeek become more advanced, questions about autonomy and decision-making authority become increasingly pressing. Should AI systems be allowed to make decisions independently, or should humans always retain control?

Levels of Autonomy

AI systems can operate at varying levels of autonomy, from fully human-controlled to fully autonomous. DeepSeek is designed to operate primarily as a decision-support tool, providing recommendations and insights while leaving final decisions to humans.

For example, in healthcare, DeepSeek can analyze medical data and suggest diagnoses or treatment options, but the ultimate decision rests with the doctor. This approach ensures that human judgment and ethical considerations remain central to the decision-making process.

The Risks of Full Autonomy

Fully autonomous AI systems pose significant ethical risks, particularly in high-stakes applications like military drones or self-driving cars. If an autonomous system makes a mistake, who is accountable? How do we ensure that the system's decisions align with human values?

DeepSeek's developers have chosen to avoid full autonomy in critical applications, prioritizing human oversight and accountability. This decision reflects a commitment to ethical principles and a recognition of the limitations of current AI technology.

The Role of Human Oversight

Human oversight is essential to ensure that AI systems like DeepSeek operate ethically and responsibly. This oversight can take many forms, from ethical review boards to real-time monitoring of AI decisions.

For example, DeepSeek's development process includes regular audits by independent ethics committees, which evaluate the system's impact on society and recommend improvements. This ongoing oversight helps ensure that DeepSeek remains aligned with human values and ethical standards.

1.3 Ensuring Transparency in AI Decision-Making

Transparency is a cornerstone of ethical AI development. Without transparency, it is impossible to understand how AI systems make decisions, assess their fairness, or hold them accountable.

Explainable AI

DeepSeek incorporates explainable AI techniques that provide insights into its decision-making process. These techniques generate human-readable explanations for the system's predictions, helping users understand how and why a particular decision was made.

For example, in a loan approval application, DeepSeek can explain which factors (e.g., income, credit history) influenced its decision and how they were weighted. This transparency builds trust and enables users to identify and address potential biases.

Open-Source Development

Another way DeepSeek promotes transparency is through open-source development. By making parts of its code and algorithms publicly available, DeepSeek invites scrutiny and collaboration from the broader AI community.

This openness not only enhances the system's reliability and security but also fosters a culture of accountability and shared responsibility.

Transparency vs. Proprietary Interests

Balancing transparency with proprietary interests can be challenging, as companies may be reluctant to reveal trade secrets or competitive advantages. DeepSeek addresses this by providing transparency at the level of decision-making processes while protecting sensitive intellectual property.

For example, while the underlying algorithms may remain proprietary, the system's decision-making criteria and ethical guidelines are made accessible to users and regulators.

Section 2: Privacy and Security Concerns

The widespread adoption of AI systems like DeepSeek raises significant concerns about privacy and security. How do we protect sensitive data while harnessing the power of AI?

2.1 Data Privacy in the Age of AI

AI systems rely on vast amounts of data to function effectively, but this reliance raises important privacy concerns.

Data Collection and Consent

DeepSeek's developers prioritize data privacy by ensuring that data collection is transparent and consensual. Users are informed about what data is being collected, how it will be used, and who will have access to it.

For example, in healthcare applications, patients must provide explicit consent before their data is used to train DeepSeek's algorithms. This approach respects individual autonomy and builds trust.

Anonymization and Encryption

To protect privacy, DeepSeek employs advanced anonymization and encryption techniques. These measures ensure that sensitive data cannot be traced back to individuals, even if it is intercepted or accessed without authorization.

For instance, in a clinical trial, patient data is anonymized before being used to train DeepSeek's models. This protects patient privacy while enabling valuable research.

The Challenge of Re-Identification

Despite these measures, the risk of re-identification remains a concern. Advances in data analytics and machine learning have made it possible to re-identify individuals from anonymized data, particularly when multiple datasets are combined.

DeepSeek addresses this challenge by implementing strict data access controls and regularly auditing its privacy practices.

2.2 Cybersecurity Threats and Safeguards

As AI systems become more integrated into critical infrastructure, they also become targets for cyberattacks.

Vulnerabilities in AI Systems

AI systems like DeepSeek are vulnerable to a range of cyber threats, including data breaches, adversarial attacks, and model poisoning. These threats can compromise the system's integrity, reliability, and safety.

For example, an adversarial attack could manipulate DeepSeek's input data to produce incorrect outputs, potentially causing harm in applications like healthcare or autonomous driving.

Robust Security Measures

To mitigate these risks, DeepSeek incorporates robust cybersecurity measures, including encryption, intrusion detection systems, and regular security audits. The system is also designed to detect and respond to anomalies in real time, minimizing the impact of potential attacks.

The Role of Human Vigilance

While technological safeguards are essential, human vigilance is equally important. DeepSeek's developers work closely with cybersecurity experts to identify and address emerging threats, ensuring that the system remains secure in an ever-evolving threat landscape.

2.3 The Role of Regulation in AI Development

Regulation plays a critical role in ensuring that AI systems like DeepSeek are developed and deployed responsibly.

Current Regulatory Frameworks

Existing regulations, such as the General Data Protection Regulation (GDPR) in the European Union, provide a foundation for protecting privacy and ensuring accountability in AI development. However, these frameworks are often limited in scope and may not fully address the unique challenges posed by AI.

The Need for AI-Specific Regulation

There is growing recognition of the need for AI-specific regulation that addresses issues like transparency, accountability, and bias. DeepSeek's developers actively engage with policymakers to advocate for such regulations, which they believe are essential for building public trust and ensuring ethical AI development.

Balancing Regulation and Innovation

While regulation is necessary, it must be carefully balanced to avoid stifling innovation. DeepSeek's developers support a collaborative approach to regulation, where industry, government, and civil society work together to create frameworks that promote both innovation and ethical responsibility.

Section 3: Addressing Bias and Inequality

AI systems like DeepSeek have the potential to exacerbate existing biases and inequalities if not developed and deployed carefully.

3.1 The Challenge of Algorithmic Bias

Algorithmic bias occurs when AI systems produce unfair or discriminatory outcomes, often as a result of biased training data or flawed algorithms.

Identifying and Mitigating Bias

DeepSeek incorporates bias detection and mitigation techniques to ensure that its decisions are fair and unbiased. These techniques include analyzing training data for patterns of bias, adjusting algorithms to minimize disparities, and conducting regular audits to evaluate the system's performance across different demographic groups.

For example, in a hiring application, DeepSeek's algorithms are designed to ignore protected attributes like gender and race, ensuring that candidates are evaluated solely on their qualifications.

The Limits of Technical Solutions

While technical solutions are important, they are not sufficient to address algorithmic bias. DeepSeek's developers recognize the need for a holistic approach that includes diverse teams, inclusive design practices, and ongoing engagement with affected communities.

3.2 AI's Impact on Employment and the Workforce

The widespread adoption of AI has the potential to disrupt labor markets and exacerbate economic inequality.

Job Displacement and Creation

While AI can automate routine tasks and increase efficiency, it can also lead to job displacement in certain industries. DeepSeek's developers are committed to mitigating these impacts by investing in reskilling and upskilling programs that prepare workers for the jobs of the future.

For example, DeepSeek has partnered with educational institutions to develop training programs in data science, AI ethics, and other high-demand fields.

The Role of Universal Basic Income

Some experts have proposed universal basic income (UBI) as a solution to the economic disruptions caused by AI. While DeepSeek's developers support exploring innovative solutions like UBI, they also emphasize the importance of creating new opportunities for meaningful work.

3.3 Bridging the Digital Divide with Inclusive AI

AI has the potential to exacerbate the digital divide, where marginalized communities lack access to technology and its benefits.

Ensuring Equitable Access

DeepSeek's developers are committed to ensuring that their technology is accessible to all, regardless of socioeconomic status. This includes developing low-cost solutions, partnering with community organizations, and advocating for policies that promote digital inclusion.

AI for Social Good

DeepSeek is also being used to address social challenges and promote equity. For example, the system has been deployed in underserved communities to improve access to healthcare, education, and financial services.

Chapter 5: DeepSeek and the Future of Work

DeepSeek AI is revolutionizing industries by automating complex tasks, enhancing decision-making, and driving unprecedented efficiency. Its advanced intelligence is transforming healthcare, finance, manufacturing, and more, reducing reliance on human labor while creating new opportunities. As AI reshapes the workforce, adaptability and innovation become key to thriving in this era of rapid technological evolution..

Section 1: Automation and Job Disruption

1.1 The Rise of AI-Driven Automation

The rise of AI-driven automation, spearheaded by systems like DeepSeek, marks a pivotal shift in how industries operate. Automation is no longer limited to repetitive, manual tasks; it now encompasses complex decision-making processes, predictive analytics, and even creative endeavors. DeepSeek's advanced neural networks and machine learning algorithms enable it to process vast amounts of data, identify patterns, and execute tasks with unparalleled precision.

For example, in manufacturing, DeepSeek-powered robots can assemble products with near-perfect accuracy, reducing errors and increasing production speed. In logistics, AI algorithms optimize supply chains by predicting demand fluctuations, minimizing waste, and streamlining inventory management. These advancements have led to significant cost savings and efficiency gains for businesses.

However, the rise of automation has also sparked concerns about job displacement. As machines take over tasks traditionally performed by humans, the workforce faces unprecedented challenges. While automation boosts productivity and reduces costs for businesses, it also raises questions about the future of employment and the skills workers will need to thrive in an AI-driven economy.

The key to addressing these challenges lies in understanding the dual nature of automation: while it eliminates certain jobs, it also creates new opportunities. By embracing automation as a tool to enhance human capabilities, we can unlock its full potential and build a more resilient workforce.

1.2 Jobs at Risk: Industries Most Affected

The impact of AI-driven automation is not uniform across industries. Some sectors are more vulnerable to disruption than others, particularly those that rely heavily on routine, predictable tasks.

- **Manufacturing and Logistics:** These industries have already seen significant automation, with robots and AI systems handling tasks like assembly, packaging, and transportation. DeepSeek's advanced robotics and predictive analytics are further accelerating this trend, reducing the need for human labor in these areas. For instance, autonomous vehicles powered by DeepSeek's AI are revolutionizing the logistics industry, enabling faster and more efficient delivery of goods.

- **Retail and Customer Service:** AI-powered chatbots and virtual assistants, like those developed by DeepSeek, are transforming customer service. These systems can handle inquiries, process orders, and resolve issues without human intervention, leading to a decline in demand for traditional customer service roles. However, they also free up human agents to focus on more complex and emotionally nuanced interactions.

- **Administrative and Clerical Work:** Tasks such as data entry, scheduling, and document processing are increasingly being automated. DeepSeek's natural language processing capabilities enable it to handle these tasks more efficiently than humans, reducing the need for administrative staff. For example, AI-powered tools can automatically generate reports, manage calendars, and even draft emails, saving time and reducing errors.

While these changes are inevitable, they also present an opportunity to rethink the role of humans in the workforce. Rather than viewing automation as a threat, we can embrace it as a tool to enhance human capabilities and create new opportunities.

1.3 New Opportunities: Jobs Created by AI

While automation may displace certain jobs, it also creates new ones. The rise of AI systems like DeepSeek has led to the emergence of entirely new industries and job roles.

- **AI Development and Maintenance:** As AI systems become more sophisticated, there is a growing demand for professionals who can design, develop, and maintain these systems. Roles such as AI engineers, data scientists, and machine learning specialists are in high demand. These professionals are responsible for building and optimizing AI algorithms, ensuring that they perform effectively and ethically.

- **AI Ethics and Governance:** The ethical implications of AI have sparked a need for experts who can ensure that AI systems are developed and deployed responsibly. Ethicists, policy analysts, and compliance officers play a crucial role in shaping the future of AI. They work to address issues such as bias, transparency, and accountability, ensuring that AI benefits society as a whole.

- **Human-AI Collaboration:** As AI takes over routine tasks, there is a growing need for roles that require human creativity, empathy, and critical thinking. Jobs in fields like healthcare, education, and the arts are becoming increasingly important, as they involve tasks that AI cannot easily replicate. For example, while AI can assist in diagnosing diseases, it is the human doctor who provides the empathy and personalized care that patients need.

DeepSeek is not just a disruptor; it is also a catalyst for innovation. By automating mundane tasks, it frees up human workers to focus on higher-value activities, driving economic growth and creating new opportunities for employment.

Section 2: Human-AI Collaboration

2.1 Augmenting Human Capabilities with AI

One of the most exciting aspects of DeepSeek is its potential to augment human capabilities. Rather than replacing humans, AI can serve as a powerful tool to enhance our skills and productivity.

In healthcare, for example, DeepSeek's diagnostic algorithms assist doctors in identifying diseases with greater accuracy and speed. By analyzing medical images and patient data, AI systems can provide insights that complement the expertise of healthcare professionals, leading to better patient outcomes. For instance, DeepSeek's AI can detect early signs of diseases like cancer, enabling timely intervention and improving survival rates.

In creative industries, DeepSeek is being used as a collaborator rather than a competitor. Musicians, writers, and artists are leveraging AI to generate new ideas, explore unconventional techniques, and push the boundaries of their craft. For instance, DeepSeek's generative AI models can compose music, write stories, and create visual art, providing inspiration and expanding the creative possibilities for human artists.

This collaborative approach to AI is transforming the way we work. By combining the strengths of humans and machines, we can achieve outcomes that neither could accomplish alone.

2.2 The Role of Creativity and Emotional Intelligence

While AI excels at tasks that involve data processing and pattern recognition, it struggles with creativity and emotional intelligence—areas where humans have a distinct advantage.

Creativity involves the ability to think outside the box, make unexpected connections, and generate novel ideas. Emotional intelligence, on the other hand, involves understanding and responding to the emotions of others, a skill that is crucial in fields like healthcare, education, and customer service.

DeepSeek's role in these areas is to support and enhance human creativity and emotional intelligence, not replace them. For example, in education, AI-powered tools can personalize learning experiences, adapting to the needs and preferences of individual students. However, it is the human teacher who provides the empathy, motivation, and mentorship that students need to thrive.

Similarly, in customer service, AI chatbots can handle routine inquiries, but human agents are still needed to address complex issues and provide a personalized touch. By leveraging the strengths of both humans and AI, we can create a more effective and empathetic workforce.

2.3 Building Trust Between Humans and Machines

Trust is a critical factor in the successful integration of AI into the workforce. For humans to collaborate effectively with AI systems like DeepSeek, they need to trust that these systems are reliable, transparent, and aligned with their values.

Building trust in AI requires addressing several key challenges:

- **Transparency:** AI systems must be able to explain their decisions in a way that humans can understand. DeepSeek's developers have prioritized explainability, ensuring that its algorithms provide clear and interpretable outputs.
- **Fairness:** AI systems must be free from bias and discrimination. DeepSeek's training processes include rigorous testing and validation to ensure that its algorithms are fair and unbiased.
- **Accountability:** There must be mechanisms in place to hold AI systems accountable for their actions. This includes establishing clear guidelines for the use of AI and ensuring that humans remain in control of critical decisions.

By addressing these challenges, DeepSeek is paving the way for a future where humans and machines can work together in harmony, leveraging the strengths of both to achieve shared goals.

Section 3: Preparing for the Future

3.1 Upskilling and Reskilling the Workforce

As AI-driven automation transforms the workforce, upskilling and reskilling have become essential for ensuring that workers can adapt to the changing landscape.

Upskilling involves teaching workers new skills that are relevant to their current roles, while reskilling involves training workers for entirely new roles. Both are critical for helping workers stay competitive in an AI-driven economy.

DeepSeek is playing a key role in this process by providing AI-powered training platforms that personalize learning experiences and adapt to the needs of individual learners. These platforms can identify skill gaps, recommend relevant courses, and track progress, making it easier for workers to acquire the skills they need to succeed.

3.2 The Role of Education in an AI-Driven World

The rise of AI is also transforming the education system. To prepare students for the future of work, schools and universities must incorporate AI literacy into their curricula.

This includes teaching students how to work with AI systems, understand their capabilities and limitations, and apply them in real-world scenarios. It also involves fostering skills like critical thinking, creativity, and emotional intelligence, which are essential for thriving in an AI-driven world.

DeepSeek is collaborating with educational institutions to develop AI-powered tools that enhance learning and teaching. For example, AI tutors can provide personalized feedback to students, while AI-driven analytics can help educators identify areas where students need additional support.

3.3 Policy Recommendations for a Balanced Future

To ensure that the benefits of AI are shared by all, policymakers must take a proactive approach to regulating AI and addressing its societal impacts.

Key policy recommendations include:

- **Investing in Education and Training:** Governments should invest in programs that help workers acquire the skills they need to thrive in an AI-driven economy.
- **Promoting Ethical AI Development:** Policymakers should establish guidelines for the ethical development and deployment of AI, ensuring that these systems are transparent, fair, and accountable.
- **Supporting Job Creation:** Governments should incentivize the creation of new jobs in emerging industries, such as AI development, renewable energy, and healthcare.

By taking these steps, we can create a future where AI enhances human potential, rather than displacing it.

Chapter 6: DeepSeek's Global Impact

The advent of artificial intelligence (AI) has ushered in a new era of technological innovation, reshaping economies, cultures, and societies across the globe. Among the leading forces in this transformation is DeepSeek, a pioneering AI company that has not only advanced the frontiers of AI research but also demonstrated the profound potential of AI to influence the world. This chapter explores the worldwide impact of DeepSeek, focusing on its role in driving economic growth, fostering cultural and social shifts, and shaping geopolitical dynamics. By examining these dimensions, we gain a comprehensive understanding of how DeepSeek is contributing to the global AI revolution and its implications for the future.

Section 1: Economic Transformation

1.1 AI as a Driver of Economic Growth

Artificial intelligence has emerged as a key driver of economic growth in the 21st century. By automating processes, enhancing productivity, and enabling new business models, AI is transforming industries and creating unprecedented opportunities for innovation. DeepSeek has been at the forefront of this transformation, leveraging its cutting-edge AI technologies to empower businesses, governments, and individuals.

One of the most significant contributions of AI to economic growth is its ability to optimize resource allocation and improve efficiency. DeepSeek's AI-powered solutions, such as predictive analytics and machine learning algorithms, have enabled companies to make data-driven decisions, reduce operational costs, and maximize profits. For example, in the manufacturing sector, DeepSeek's AI systems have streamlined supply chains, minimized waste, and accelerated production cycles, leading to significant economic gains.

Moreover, AI has opened up new avenues for entrepreneurship and job creation. DeepSeek's platforms have democratized access to AI tools, enabling startups and small businesses to compete with established players. By providing affordable and scalable AI solutions, DeepSeek has fostered innovation in emerging industries such as fintech, healthcare, and renewable energy. This has not only stimulated economic growth but also created millions of jobs worldwide.

However, the economic impact of AI is not without challenges. The displacement of workers due to automation has raised concerns about job losses and income inequality. DeepSeek has addressed these challenges by investing in reskilling and upskilling programs, ensuring that workers are equipped with the skills needed to thrive in the AI-driven economy. Through partnerships with educational institutions and governments, DeepSeek has played a pivotal role in preparing the global workforce for the future of work.

1.2 DeepSeek's Role in Emerging Markets

Emerging markets have been among the greatest beneficiaries of DeepSeek's AI technologies. By addressing critical challenges such as infrastructure gaps, limited access to healthcare, and financial exclusion, DeepSeek has empowered these regions to leapfrog traditional development pathways and achieve sustainable growth.

In Africa, for instance, DeepSeek's AI-powered healthcare solutions have revolutionized the delivery of medical services. By leveraging telemedicine and diagnostic algorithms, DeepSeek has enabled remote communities to access quality healthcare, reducing the burden on overstretched healthcare systems. Similarly, in Southeast Asia, DeepSeek's fintech platforms have expanded financial inclusion, providing millions of unbanked individuals with access to credit, savings, and insurance.

DeepSeek's impact on agriculture in emerging markets has also been transformative. By deploying AI-driven precision farming techniques, DeepSeek has helped farmers increase crop yields, reduce resource consumption, and adapt to climate change. This has not only improved food security but also boosted rural economies, lifting millions out of poverty.

The company's commitment to emerging markets extends beyond technology deployment. DeepSeek has established local research and development centers, fostering collaboration with regional stakeholders and tailoring solutions to meet the unique needs of these markets. This localized approach has enabled DeepSeek to build trust and drive adoption, ensuring that the benefits of AI are equitably distributed.

1.3 The Global AI Race: Competition and Collaboration

The rapid advancement of AI has sparked a global race for dominance, with nations and corporations vying to establish leadership in this transformative technology. DeepSeek has emerged as a key player in this race, competing with tech giants and startups alike to push the boundaries of AI innovation.

The competition in the AI landscape has driven significant investments in research and development, accelerating the pace of technological progress. DeepSeek's breakthroughs in natural language processing, computer vision, and reinforcement learning have set new benchmarks for the industry, inspiring competitors to raise their game. This healthy competition has fueled a virtuous cycle of innovation, benefiting society as a whole.

At the same time, DeepSeek has recognized the importance of collaboration in addressing the complex challenges posed by AI. The company has actively participated in global initiatives aimed at promoting ethical AI development, sharing best practices, and establishing common standards. By collaborating with governments, academia, and civil society, DeepSeek has contributed to the creation of a more inclusive and sustainable AI ecosystem.

The global AI race has also highlighted the need for international cooperation in areas such as data governance, cybersecurity, and intellectual property rights. DeepSeek has advocated for multilateral approaches to these issues, emphasizing the importance of balancing competition with collaboration to ensure that AI serves the greater good.

Section 2: Cultural and Social Shifts

2.1 How AI is Changing the Way We Live

The influence of AI extends far beyond the economic sphere, permeating every aspect of our daily lives. DeepSeek's technologies have played a central role in shaping cultural and social norms, redefining how we communicate, learn, and interact with the world around us.

One of the most visible impacts of AI is its transformation of the media and entertainment industry. DeepSeek's content recommendation algorithms have revolutionized the way we consume information, enabling personalized experiences that cater to individual preferences. This has not only enhanced user engagement but also raised questions about the role of AI in shaping public opinion and cultural narratives.

In education, DeepSeek's AI-powered platforms have democratized access to knowledge, breaking down barriers of geography and socioeconomic status. Adaptive learning systems developed by DeepSeek have personalized education, enabling students to learn at their own pace and achieve better outcomes. This has the potential to bridge the global education gap, empowering individuals to unlock their full potential.

AI has also transformed the way we interact with technology. DeepSeek's virtual assistants and chatbots have become integral parts of our lives, simplifying tasks and providing instant access to information. These AI-driven interfaces have not only enhanced convenience but also reshaped social dynamics, influencing how we communicate and build relationships.

2.2 The Role of AI in Addressing Global Challenges

DeepSeek's AI technologies have proven to be powerful tools in addressing some of the world's most pressing challenges. From climate change to public health, AI is enabling innovative solutions that were once thought impossible.

In the fight against climate change, DeepSeek's AI models have been instrumental in predicting environmental trends, optimizing energy consumption, and developing sustainable practices. For example, DeepSeek's AI-powered climate simulations have provided policymakers with actionable insights, enabling them to design effective mitigation strategies. Similarly, the company's smart grid technologies have facilitated the integration of renewable energy sources, reducing reliance on fossil fuels.

The COVID-19 pandemic underscored the importance of AI in public health. DeepSeek's AI-driven diagnostic tools and vaccine development platforms played a critical role in combating the virus, saving countless lives. The company's data analytics capabilities also enabled governments to track the spread of the virus and implement targeted interventions, demonstrating the potential of AI to enhance global health security.

2.3 Ethical and Cultural Considerations Across Borders

As AI becomes increasingly pervasive, it has raised important ethical and cultural questions that transcend national boundaries. DeepSeek has been at the forefront of efforts to address these concerns, advocating for responsible AI development that respects diverse cultural values and human rights.

One of the key ethical challenges posed by AI is the issue of bias. DeepSeek has implemented rigorous measures to ensure that its algorithms are fair and unbiased, conducting regular audits and incorporating diverse datasets. The company has also engaged with stakeholders from different cultural backgrounds to understand their perspectives and incorporate them into its AI systems.

Privacy is another critical concern in the age of AI. DeepSeek has prioritized data protection, developing robust encryption and anonymization techniques to safeguard user information. The company has also supported the development of global privacy standards, ensuring that individuals retain control over their data.

Cultural considerations are equally important in the deployment of AI technologies. DeepSeek has recognized that AI systems must be sensitive to local customs and traditions, avoiding the imposition of foreign values. By fostering cross-cultural dialogue and collaboration, DeepSeek has ensured that its technologies are inclusive and respectful of cultural diversity.

Section 3: Geopolitical Implications

3.1 AI as a Tool for National Security

The strategic importance of AI has made it a focal point of national security policies worldwide. DeepSeek's advancements in AI have positioned it as a key player in this domain, providing governments with tools to enhance their defense capabilities and protect their citizens.

AI-powered surveillance systems developed by DeepSeek have enabled governments to monitor threats in real time, improving their ability to respond to emergencies. The company's cybersecurity solutions have also been instrumental in safeguarding critical infrastructure from cyberattacks, ensuring national security in an increasingly digital world.

However, the use of AI in national security has raised ethical and legal concerns. DeepSeek has advocated for the responsible use of AI in defense, emphasizing the importance of transparency, accountability, and adherence to international law. The company has also called for the establishment of global norms to govern the use of AI in military applications, preventing an arms race that could destabilize the world.

3.2 The Role of AI in Diplomacy and International Relations

AI is reshaping the landscape of diplomacy and international relations, providing new tools for communication, negotiation, and conflict resolution. DeepSeek's AI-powered translation and sentiment analysis tools have facilitated cross-cultural dialogue, enabling diplomats to bridge linguistic and cultural divides.

The company's predictive analytics capabilities have also enhanced the ability of governments to anticipate global trends and make informed decisions. By analyzing vast amounts of data, DeepSeek's AI systems have provided insights into geopolitical dynamics, helping policymakers navigate complex international issues.

AI has also opened up new avenues for international cooperation. DeepSeek has participated in global initiatives aimed at addressing shared challenges such as climate change, pandemics, and cybersecurity. By fostering collaboration among nations, DeepSeek has demonstrated the potential of AI to promote peace and stability.

3.3 Balancing Power in the AI Era

The rise of AI has significant implications for the global balance of power, with nations competing to establish dominance in this critical technology. DeepSeek's leadership in AI has positioned it as a key player in this geopolitical contest, influencing the distribution of power in the AI era.

The company's global reach and technological prowess have enabled it to shape the rules of the AI landscape, setting standards that others must follow. DeepSeek's commitment to ethical AI development has also given it a moral authority, allowing it to influence global discourse on AI governance.

At the same time, DeepSeek has recognized the importance of maintaining a balance of power in the AI era. The company has advocated for multilateral approaches to AI governance, ensuring that no single nation or entity dominates the technology. By promoting inclusivity and cooperation, DeepSeek has sought to create a more equitable and sustainable AI ecosystem.

Chapter 7: The Road Ahead for DeepSeek

As DeepSeek continues to evolve, the road ahead is both exhilarating and daunting. The future of artificial intelligence (AI) is a landscape filled with immense potential, but it is also riddled with challenges that must be navigated with care. This chapter delves into the emerging technologies that will shape DeepSeek's trajectory, the challenges that lie ahead, and the vision for a future where DeepSeek plays a pivotal role in transforming the world.

Section 1: Emerging Technologies

1.1 Quantum Computing and AI

Quantum computing represents a paradigm shift in computational power, offering the potential to solve problems that are currently intractable for classical computers. For DeepSeek, the integration of quantum computing with AI could unlock unprecedented capabilities.

Quantum Supremacy and AI: Quantum supremacy, the point at which quantum computers can perform tasks that classical computers cannot, could revolutionize AI. Quantum algorithms, such as Grover's and Shor's, could exponentially speed up data processing, optimization, and machine learning tasks. DeepSeek could leverage quantum computing to enhance its natural language processing, predictive analytics, and decision-making algorithms, making them more efficient and accurate.

Quantum Machine Learning: Quantum machine learning (QML) is an emerging field that combines quantum computing with machine learning techniques. QML could enable DeepSeek to process vast datasets more efficiently, uncover hidden patterns, and develop more sophisticated models. For instance, quantum-enhanced neural networks could lead to breakthroughs in image recognition, speech synthesis, and autonomous systems.

Challenges in Quantum AI: Despite its potential, quantum computing is still in its infancy. Technical challenges, such as quantum decoherence and error correction, need to be addressed before quantum AI can become a reality. DeepSeek must stay at the forefront of quantum research, collaborating with leading quantum computing labs and investing in quantum-ready infrastructure.

1.2 The Integration of AI with Other Cutting-Edge Technologies

The future of AI lies in its integration with other cutting-edge technologies, creating a synergistic effect that amplifies the capabilities of each. DeepSeek is poised to be at the forefront of this convergence.

AI and the Internet of Things (IoT): The IoT ecosystem, with its billions of connected devices, generates vast amounts of data. DeepSeek can harness this data to create intelligent systems that optimize energy consumption, improve healthcare, and enhance urban planning. For example, AI-driven IoT systems could predict equipment failures in industrial settings, reducing downtime and maintenance costs.

AI and Blockchain: Blockchain technology offers a decentralized and secure way to store and share data. DeepSeek can integrate AI with blockchain to create transparent and tamper-proof AI models. This integration could be particularly valuable in industries like finance, where AI-driven blockchain systems could detect fraudulent transactions in real-time.

AI and Augmented Reality (AR): AR overlays digital information onto the physical world, creating immersive experiences. DeepSeek can leverage AI to enhance AR applications, such as virtual assistants that provide real-time information and guidance. In healthcare, AI-powered AR could assist surgeons by overlaying critical patient data during procedures.

AI and Biotechnology: The intersection of AI and biotechnology holds immense promise for personalized medicine, drug discovery, and genetic engineering. DeepSeek can develop AI models that analyze genomic data to identify potential treatments for diseases, predict patient outcomes, and optimize drug development processes.

1.3 The Next Frontier: General AI

While DeepSeek has made significant strides in narrow AI, the ultimate goal is to achieve General AI (AGI) – AI that possesses human-like cognitive abilities and can perform any intellectual task that a human can.

Defining AGI: AGI represents a level of AI that can understand, learn, and apply knowledge across a wide range of domains. Unlike narrow AI, which is designed for specific tasks, AGI can generalize its learning to new situations, making it more versatile and adaptable.

The Path to AGI: Achieving AGI requires advancements in several areas, including neural architecture, learning algorithms, and computational power. DeepSeek must focus on developing more sophisticated neural networks that can mimic the human brain's ability to process and integrate information from multiple sources. Reinforcement learning, unsupervised learning, and transfer learning are key areas of research that could bring us closer to AGI.

Ethical Considerations: The development of AGI raises profound ethical questions. How do we ensure that AGI aligns with human values and goals? What safeguards are needed to prevent AGI from being used for malicious purposes? DeepSeek must engage with ethicists, policymakers, and the broader AI community to address these concerns and develop ethical guidelines for AGI development.

The Impact of AGI: The advent of AGI could transform every aspect of society, from healthcare and education to transportation and entertainment. DeepSeek envisions a future where AGI collaborates with humans to solve complex global challenges, such as climate change, poverty, and disease. However, the realization of this vision requires careful planning and collaboration to ensure that AGI benefits all of humanity.

Section 2: Challenges to Overcome

2.1 Technical Limitations and Bottlenecks

Despite the rapid advancements in AI, several technical limitations and bottlenecks must be addressed to unlock its full potential.

Computational Power: AI models, particularly deep learning models, require vast amounts of computational power. Training these models can be resource-intensive, requiring specialized hardware like

GPUs and TPUs. As AI models become more complex, the demand for computational resources will only increase. DeepSeek must invest in scalable infrastructure and explore alternative computing paradigms, such as neuromorphic computing, to meet this demand.

Data Quality and Availability: AI models are only as good as the data they are trained on. Poor-quality data, biased datasets, and data scarcity can limit the effectiveness of AI systems. DeepSeek must prioritize data quality and invest in data collection, cleaning, and augmentation techniques. Additionally, the company should explore federated learning and synthetic data generation to overcome data scarcity issues.

Model Interpretability: As AI models become more complex, they often become "black boxes," making it difficult to understand how they arrive at their decisions. This lack of interpretability can be a barrier to adoption, particularly in high-stakes applications like healthcare and finance. DeepSeek must focus on developing explainable AI (XAI) techniques that provide transparency and accountability in AI decision-making.

Scalability and Deployment: Deploying AI models at scale presents numerous challenges, including model optimization, latency, and integration with existing systems. DeepSeek must develop robust deployment pipelines that ensure AI models can be seamlessly integrated into real-world applications. Additionally, the company should explore edge computing to enable AI processing at the source of data generation, reducing latency and bandwidth requirements.

2.2 Ethical and Regulatory Hurdles

As AI becomes more pervasive, it raises a host of ethical and regulatory challenges that must be addressed to ensure its responsible use.

Bias and Fairness: AI models can inadvertently perpetuate and amplify biases present in the training data, leading to unfair and discriminatory outcomes. DeepSeek must implement rigorous bias detection and mitigation techniques to ensure that its AI systems are fair and equitable. This includes diverse dataset collection, algorithmic audits, and continuous monitoring of AI outputs.

Privacy and Security: The widespread use of AI raises concerns about data privacy and security. AI systems often require access to sensitive personal data, making them potential targets for cyberattacks. DeepSeek must prioritize data protection by implementing robust encryption, anonymization, and access control measures. Additionally, the company should advocate for privacy-preserving AI techniques, such as differential privacy and homomorphic encryption.

Accountability and Transparency: As AI systems make increasingly consequential decisions, questions of accountability and transparency become paramount. Who is responsible when an AI system makes a mistake? How can we ensure that AI decisions are transparent and understandable? DeepSeek must work with regulators, industry stakeholders, and the public to establish clear guidelines for AI accountability and transparency.

Regulatory Compliance: The regulatory landscape for AI is still evolving, with different countries and regions adopting varying approaches to AI governance. DeepSeek must navigate this complex regulatory environment by staying informed about emerging laws and regulations, engaging with policymakers, and advocating for balanced and effective AI governance frameworks.

2.3 Public Perception and Acceptance of AI

The success of AI depends not only on technological advancements but also on public perception and acceptance. DeepSeek must address societal concerns and build trust in AI systems.

Addressing Fear and Misconceptions: AI has been the subject of both hype and fear, leading to misconceptions about its capabilities and risks. DeepSeek must engage in public education and outreach to demystify AI and provide accurate information about its potential and limitations. This includes transparent communication about how AI systems work, their benefits, and the safeguards in place to prevent misuse.

Building Trust: Trust is a critical factor in the adoption of AI. DeepSeek must demonstrate its commitment to ethical AI practices by being transparent about its development processes, data usage, and decision-making criteria. The company should also establish mechanisms for public feedback and accountability, ensuring that AI systems are aligned with societal values.

Inclusive AI Development: AI systems should be designed with inclusivity in mind, ensuring that they benefit all segments of society. DeepSeek must prioritize diversity and inclusion in its AI development teams, ensuring that a wide range of perspectives are considered in the design and deployment of AI systems. Additionally, the company should engage with underrepresented communities to understand their needs and concerns, ensuring that AI solutions are equitable and accessible.

Ethical AI Leadership: As a leader in the AI industry, DeepSeek has a responsibility to set an example for ethical AI development. The company should actively participate in industry initiatives, collaborate with academic institutions, and contribute to the development of ethical AI standards and best practices. By leading by example, DeepSeek can help shape the future of AI in a way that is responsible, ethical, and beneficial to all.

Section 3: Vision for the Future

3.1 DeepSeek's Long-Term Goals and Aspirations

DeepSeek's long-term vision is to create AI systems that enhance human capabilities, solve complex global challenges, and improve the quality of life for people around the world. This vision is guided by several key goals and aspirations.

Advancing AI Research: DeepSeek is committed to pushing the boundaries of AI research, exploring new frontiers in machine learning, natural language processing, computer vision, and beyond. The company aims to develop AI systems that are not only more powerful but also more ethical, transparent, and aligned with human values.

Solving Global Challenges: DeepSeek envisions a future where AI plays a central role in addressing some of the world's most pressing challenges, such as climate change, healthcare, education, and poverty. By leveraging AI's predictive and analytical capabilities, DeepSeek aims to develop solutions that are scalable, sustainable, and impactful.

Empowering Individuals and Communities: DeepSeek's mission is to empower individuals and communities by making AI accessible and beneficial to all. The company is committed to developing AI tools and platforms that are user-friendly, inclusive, and designed to enhance human creativity, productivity, and well-being.

Fostering Innovation and Collaboration: DeepSeek believes that the future of AI lies in collaboration and innovation. The company aims to foster a culture of openness, collaboration, and knowledge-sharing, both within the organization and with the broader AI community. By working together, DeepSeek and its partners can accelerate the development of AI technologies and ensure that they are used for the greater good.

3.2 The Role of Collaboration in Advancing AI

Collaboration is essential for advancing AI and ensuring that it benefits society as a whole. DeepSeek recognizes the importance of working with a diverse range of stakeholders, including academia, industry, government, and civil society.

Academic Partnerships: DeepSeek collaborates with leading academic institutions to advance AI research and education. These partnerships enable the company to stay at the cutting edge of AI innovation, access top talent, and contribute to the development of the next generation of AI researchers and practitioners.

Industry Collaboration: DeepSeek works with industry partners to develop and deploy AI solutions that address real-world challenges. By collaborating with companies across different sectors, DeepSeek can leverage its AI expertise to create value and drive innovation in areas such as healthcare, finance, manufacturing, and transportation.

Government Engagement: DeepSeek engages with governments and policymakers to shape the regulatory landscape for AI. The company advocates for policies that promote innovation while ensuring that AI is developed and used responsibly. DeepSeek also collaborates with governments on AI initiatives that address societal challenges, such as public health, safety, and security.

Civil Society and Ethical AI: DeepSeek recognizes the importance of engaging with civil society organizations to ensure that AI development is guided by ethical principles and societal values. The company works with NGOs, advocacy groups, and community organizations to understand the impact of AI on different communities and to develop AI solutions that are inclusive and equitable.

3.3 Envisioning a World Transformed by DeepSeek

DeepSeek envisions a future where AI is seamlessly integrated into every aspect of life, enhancing human capabilities and creating new opportunities for growth and innovation.

AI in Everyday Life: In the future, AI will be an invisible yet omnipresent force, enhancing our daily lives in ways we can hardly imagine. From personalized healthcare and education to smart homes and cities, AI will make our lives more convenient, efficient, and enjoyable. DeepSeek's AI systems will be at the heart of this transformation, providing intelligent solutions that adapt to our needs and preferences.

AI and the Future of Work: AI will revolutionize the way we work, automating routine tasks and enabling us to focus on more creative and strategic activities. DeepSeek's AI tools will empower workers across industries, from healthcare professionals and educators to engineers and artists. By augmenting human capabilities, AI will create new job opportunities and drive economic growth.

AI and Global Challenges: DeepSeek's AI systems will play a crucial role in addressing global challenges, such as climate change, food security, and public health. By analyzing vast amounts of data and identifying patterns and trends, AI will enable us to make more informed decisions and take proactive measures to mitigate risks and seize opportunities.

AI and Human-AI Collaboration: The future of AI is not about replacing humans but about enhancing human capabilities through collaboration. DeepSeek envisions a world where humans and AI work together as partners, leveraging each other's strengths to achieve common goals. This collaborative approach will lead to more innovative solutions, better decision-making, and a more equitable and sustainable world.

AI and Ethical Responsibility: As AI becomes more pervasive, DeepSeek is committed to ensuring that its development and use are guided by ethical principles. The company will continue to prioritize transparency, fairness, and accountability in its AI systems, ensuring that they are aligned with human values and contribute to the greater good.

In conclusion, the road ahead for DeepSeek is filled with opportunities and challenges. By staying at the forefront of emerging technologies, addressing technical and ethical hurdles, and fostering collaboration, DeepSeek is poised to lead the way in shaping a future where AI transforms the world for the better. The journey ahead is long, but with a clear vision and a commitment to ethical AI, DeepSeek is ready to navigate the complexities of the AI landscape and create a brighter future for all.

Chapter 8: A Call to Action

The rapid evolution of artificial intelligence (AI) has brought us to a pivotal moment in history. AI is no longer a distant dream or a concept confined to science fiction; it is a tangible force reshaping industries, economies, and societies. As we stand on the brink of this transformative era, the question is no longer whether AI will influence our future, but how we will shape its trajectory. This chapter is a call to action—a rallying cry for individuals, communities, and organizations to actively engage with AI and ensure it serves as a force for good. The future of AI is not predetermined; it is ours to design, and the time to act is now.

Section 1: Empowering Individuals

The power to shape the future of AI begins with individuals. Each of us has a role to play in embracing this technology, advocating for its ethical use, and committing to lifelong learning. By empowering ourselves, we can collectively steer AI toward a future that benefits humanity.

1.1 How You Can Embrace AI in Your Life

AI is no longer the exclusive domain of researchers and tech giants. It has permeated everyday life, from personalized recommendations on streaming platforms to voice assistants that simplify daily tasks. Embracing AI starts with understanding its potential and integrating it into your personal and professional life.

- **Explore AI Tools**: Begin by experimenting with AI-powered tools and applications. Whether it's using language models like DeepSeek for creative writing, leveraging AI for data analysis, or adopting smart home devices, familiarity with these technologies will demystify AI and reveal its practical benefits.
- **Enhance Productivity**: AI can streamline workflows, automate repetitive tasks, and provide insights that enhance decision-making. By incorporating AI into your work, you can free up time for more creative and strategic endeavors.
- **Stay Informed**: The field of AI is evolving rapidly. Stay updated on the latest developments by following reputable news sources, attending webinars, and participating in online courses. Knowledge is the first step toward meaningful engagement.
- **Engage with the AI Community**: Join forums, attend meetups, and connect with others who share your interest in AI. Collaboration and dialogue are essential for fostering innovation and addressing challenges.
-

1.2 Becoming an Advocate for Ethical AI

As AI becomes more integrated into society, ethical considerations must take center stage. Individuals have a responsibility to advocate for AI systems that are fair, transparent, and accountable.

- **Understand the Ethical Implications**: Educate yourself about the ethical challenges posed by AI, such as bias in algorithms, privacy concerns, and the potential for job displacement. Awareness is the foundation of advocacy.
- **Demand Transparency**: Support organizations and initiatives that prioritize transparency in AI development. Encourage companies to disclose how their AI systems work and how they address ethical concerns.
- **Promote Inclusivity**: Advocate for AI systems that are inclusive and accessible to all. This includes ensuring that diverse perspectives are represented in AI development and that the benefits of AI are equitably distributed.
- **Hold Leaders Accountable**: Use your voice to hold governments, corporations, and institutions accountable for the ethical use of AI. Support policies and regulations that protect individuals and promote responsible innovation.

1.3 Lifelong Learning in the Age of AI

The rapid pace of technological change necessitates a commitment to lifelong learning. In the age of AI, staying relevant means continuously acquiring new skills and adapting to new paradigms.

- **Develop AI Literacy**: Even if you are not a technologist, understanding the basics of AI—how it works, its capabilities, and its limitations—is essential. AI literacy empowers you to make informed decisions and engage in meaningful conversations about its impact.
- **Upskill and Reskill**: As AI transforms industries, certain skills will become obsolete while others will be in high demand. Invest in upskilling (enhancing existing skills) and reskilling (learning new skills) to remain competitive in the job market.
- **Embrace a Growth Mindset**: Cultivate a mindset that embraces change and views challenges as opportunities for growth. The ability to adapt and learn will be one of the most valuable assets in the AI-driven future.
- **Leverage AI for Learning**: Use AI-powered educational platforms to personalize your learning experience. These tools can help you identify areas for improvement, recommend resources, and track your progress.

Section 2: Building a Better Future

The transformative potential of AI extends far beyond individual empowerment. It offers unprecedented opportunities to address global challenges and build a better future for all. However, realizing this potential requires innovation, collaboration, and a commitment to ensuring that AI benefits everyone.

2.1 The Role of Innovation in Solving Global Problems

AI has the power to tackle some of the world's most pressing challenges, from climate change to healthcare disparities. Innovation is the key to unlocking this potential.

- **Climate Change**: AI can optimize energy consumption, predict environmental changes, and develop sustainable solutions. For example, AI-powered models can analyze vast amounts of data to identify patterns and inform strategies for reducing carbon emissions.
- **Healthcare**: AI is revolutionizing healthcare by enabling early diagnosis, personalized treatment, and drug discovery. By leveraging AI, we can improve access to quality healthcare and address disparities in underserved communities.
- **Education**: AI can democratize education by providing personalized learning experiences and making high-quality resources accessible to learners worldwide. This has the potential to

bridge the global education gap and empower future generations.

- **Poverty and Inequality**: AI can help identify and address the root causes of poverty and inequality. For instance, AI-driven analytics can inform policies that promote economic inclusion and social justice.

2.2   Collaboration   Between   Governments, Businesses, and Communities

The complexity of global challenges requires a collaborative approach. Governments, businesses, and communities must work together to harness the power of AI for the greater good.

- **Public-Private Partnerships**: Governments and businesses can collaborate to fund AI research, develop infrastructure, and create policies that promote innovation while safeguarding public interests.
- **Community Engagement**: Local communities play a crucial role in shaping the future of AI. By involving community members in AI initiatives, we can ensure that solutions are culturally relevant and address local needs.
- **Global Cooperation**: AI is a global phenomenon that transcends borders. International cooperation is essential for establishing ethical standards, sharing

knowledge, and addressing challenges that affect humanity as a whole.

2.3 Ensuring AI Benefits All of Humanity

The benefits of AI must be distributed equitably to avoid exacerbating existing inequalities. This requires a concerted effort to ensure that AI serves all of humanity, not just a privileged few.

- **Bridging the Digital Divide**: Access to AI technologies and the internet is unevenly distributed. Efforts must be made to bridge the digital divide and ensure that everyone has the opportunity to benefit from AI.
- **Promoting Fairness and Inclusion**: AI systems must be designed to be fair and inclusive. This includes addressing biases in data and algorithms and ensuring that diverse voices are represented in AI development.
- **Protecting Vulnerable Populations**: Special attention must be given to protecting vulnerable populations, such as children, the elderly, and marginalized communities, from potential harms of AI.
- **Fostering Economic Opportunities**: AI has the potential to create new economic opportunities, but it also poses risks to jobs and livelihoods. Policies must be put in place to support workers in transitioning to new roles and industries.

Section 3: The Legacy of DeepSeek

As we reflect on the journey of AI, it is impossible to ignore the profound impact of DeepSeek. This groundbreaking AI system has not only advanced the field of artificial intelligence but also inspired a new generation of innovators and thinkers.

3.1 DeepSeek's Impact on the World

DeepSeek has revolutionized the way we interact with technology, enabling breakthroughs in fields ranging from healthcare to education. Its ability to process and analyze vast amounts of data has unlocked new possibilities for solving complex problems.

- **Transforming Industries**: DeepSeek has transformed industries by automating processes, enhancing decision-making, and driving innovation. Its applications span healthcare, finance, transportation, and beyond.
- **Empowering Individuals**: By making AI accessible and user-friendly, DeepSeek has empowered individuals to harness the power of AI in their personal and professional lives.
- **Inspiring Innovation**: DeepSeek has inspired countless individuals and organizations to explore the potential of AI and push the boundaries of what is possible.
-

3.2 Lessons Learned from the DeepSeek Journey

The development and deployment of DeepSeek offer valuable lessons for the future of AI.

- **The Importance of Ethics**: DeepSeek's commitment to ethical AI serves as a model for responsible innovation. It underscores the importance of prioritizing fairness, transparency, and accountability in AI development.
- **The Power of Collaboration**: DeepSeek's success is a testament to the power of collaboration. By bringing together diverse perspectives and expertise, we can achieve breakthroughs that would be impossible in isolation.
- **The Need for Adaptability**: The journey of DeepSeek highlights the need for adaptability in the face of rapid technological change. Staying ahead of the curve requires a willingness to learn, evolve, and embrace new challenges.

3.3 A Final Reflection: The Power of Human Ingenuity

As we look to the future, it is clear that the power of AI lies not in the technology itself, but in the human ingenuity that drives it. AI is a tool—a powerful one—but it is ultimately up to us to determine how it is used.

- **The Human Element**: Despite the advancements in AI, the human element remains irreplaceable. Creativity, empathy, and critical thinking are uniquely human traits that will continue to drive progress.
- **A Shared Responsibility**: Shaping the future of AI is a shared responsibility. Each of us has a role to play in ensuring that AI serves as a force for good.
- **A Call to Action**: The future of AI is not predetermined. It is ours to design. Let us embrace this opportunity with courage, curiosity, and a commitment to building a better world.

www.ingramcontent.com/pod-product-compliance
Lightning Source LLC
LaVergne TN
LVHW022354060326
832902LV00022B/4439